THE
COUNTRY DANCE BOOK

PART I.

CONTAINING A DESCRIPTION OF

EIGHTEEN TRADITIONAL DANCES

COLLECTED IN COUNTRY VILLAGES

BY

CECIL J. SHARP.

———

LONDON
NOVELLO AND COMPANY, Ltd.

1909

MADE IN ENGLAND.

This Book is issued in connection with "Country Dance Tunes,"
by the same Author.

(Sets I. and II., price (1/6) 3/- each.)

LONDON: NOVELLO AND COMPANY, LIMITED.

PREFACE.

THE Author desires to acknowledge his indebtedness to Mrs. Montagu Fordham, Mrs. Stanton, Miss Wyatt-Edgell, the Rev. S. Baring-Gould, and to all those who have helped him to find and to note the Country Dances described in this book. His grateful thanks are also due to Mr. William Ford, Mr. Thomas Hands, Mr. John Lavercombe, and those dancers and fiddlers from whom much of the technical information contained in the following pages has been derived.

CONTENTS.

INTRODUCTION.

Up till a few years ago it was commonly believed that the English race was the only one in Europe that was unable to make any contribution to the literature of folk-song. Opinions may still be divided as to the artistic worth of our national folk-songs, but their existence, and in great abundance, can no longer be disputed.

A similar misconception with regard to English folk-dances awaits refutation. Maybe, the contents of this volume, following upon the issue of *The Morris Book* and other similar publications, will aid in the work of enlightenment.

In justification of the attitude of apathetic indifference which, until recently, we held towards the folk-music of our own country, it should be remembered that since the days of the Restoration the musical taste of the upper classes in England has been frankly and unashamedly cosmopolitan. This strange preference for foreign music and prejudice against the native product has been, however, characteristic only of the more educated. It has never been shared by the unlettered, who have always sung the songs and danced the dances of their forefathers, uninfluenced by, and in blissful ignorance of the habits and tastes of their more fashionable city neighbours. But this is, unhappily, no longer so. The State schools, the railways, and the hundred and one causes which have led to the depopulation of the country villages are rapidly changing, some would say debasing, the taste of the present generation—of those, that is, whose ancestors were both guardians and inventors of our traditional music and national pastimes. In the village of to-day the polka, waltz, and quadrille are steadily displacing the old-time country dances and jigs, just as the tawdry ballads and strident street-songs of the towns are no less surely exterminating the folk-songs. Fortunately, there is yet time to do for the dances what has already been done so successfully for the songs, namely, to collect, publish and preserve the best of them for the benefit of our own and future generations.

But national prejudice dies hard : more especially when it is perpetually being nourished by those who profess to instruct. "We cannot now find among the rural population (of England) any traces of what may be called a national dance," says the author of a recent *History of Dancing*, one, moreover, who lived in the centre of that district where, perhaps, the old dances flourish more vigorously than anywhere else in England. A few months ago, too, the foreign correspondent of one of our chief daily journals, after giving an account of the Northern Games at Stockholm, innocently remarked :—" It would be a merrier and better England which could produce dances of this kind as a spontaneous and natural growth."

This perverse indifference to facts is all the more remarkable when we remember that in the early days of our history we were renowned throughout Europe for our dancing no less than for our singing. "In saltatione et arte musicâ excellunt" is an oft-quoted tribute paid to us by Hentzner in 1598 ; while Beaumont spoke of the delight which the Portuguese or Spaniards had in riding great horses, the French in courteous behaviour, and the " dancing English in carrying a fair presence." But there is no need to labour the point. The fact that we once held this reputation is not questioned. The error has been too readily to assume, with our author of the *History of Dancing*, that because the upper classes have forgotten their native songs and dances, the peasantry have been equally neglectful.

This is especially unfortunate, for we happen to possess in England, in the Morris and the Country Dance, two folk-dances of unusual interest, not only to the archæologist and student of social history, but to the lover of dancing also. They represent two generically distinct types, of which indeed it might be said that they differ in almost every way that once dance can differ from another.

The Morris, for instance, is a ceremonial, spectacular and professional dance ; it is performed by men only, and has no sex characteristics.

The many curious customs—as well as the extra characters, *e.g.*, the squire or fool, king, queen, witch, cake and sword bearer—which are commonly associated with the dance, all indicate that the Morris was once something more than a mere dance ; that, originally, the dance formed but one part of what may very likely have been an elaborate quasi-religious ceremony. An analysis of the figures of the dance leads to the same conclusion. This may be equally true of many of the folk-dances of other nations, but very few bear upon them, as does the Morris, such clear and unmistakable indications of derivation from the primitive nature ceremonies of the early village communities.

And these qualities, which the Morris derived from its ceremonial origin, it has never lost. As practised to-day it is, as throughout its history it has always been, a formal, official dance, performed only on certain days in each year, such as Whitsun-week, the annual club feast, wake, or fair-day.

The village Morris-men, moreover, are few in number, especially chosen and trained, and form a close society or guild of professional performers. Admission into their ranks is formal and conditioned. It is not enough that the probationer should be a good dancer, lissome and agile ; he must, in addition, undergo a course of six weeks' daily instruction at the hands of the elder dancers. Upon election, he will be required to subscribe to sundry rules and regulations, and provide himself with a special and elaborate dancing dress, every detail of which, though varying from village to village, is prescribed by tradition.

The Morris, too, is remarkable for the total absence of the

love motive from all its movements. There is scarcely a single dance in which the performers so much as touch each other, while " handing " is quite unknown.

Finally, it must be understood that the Morris is not, primarily, a pleasure dance. Its function is to provide a spectacle or pageant as part of the ritual associated with the celebration of popular festivals and holidays.

The Country Dance, on the other hand, possesses none of these special characteristics. It has played altogether another part in the social life of the village. No ceremony or formality has ever been associated with its performance. It was, and so far as it is practised it still is, the ordinary, everyday dance of the country-folk, performed not merely on festal days, but whenever opportunity offered and the spirit of merrymaking was abroad. So far from being a man's dance, it is performed in couples, or partners of opposite sexes; while flirtation or coquetry lies at the root of nearly all of its figures and evolutions. No special dress is needed, not even holiday clothes. The steps and figures are simple and easily learned, so that anyone of ordinary intelligence and of average physique can without difficulty qualify as a competent performer.

Nor has the Country Dance ever been regarded as a spectacle or pageant, like the Morris. It has always been danced purely for its own sake, for the pleasure it afforded the performers and the social intercourse that it provided. More than a hundred years ago a French author drew attention to this point in the following passage:—" Au village l'on danse pour le seul plaisir de danser, pour agiter les membres accoutumés à un violent exercice; on danse pour exhaler un sentiment de joie qui n'a pas besoin de spectateurs." The same idea was expressed by Edward Philips, Milton's nephew, in *The Mysteries of Love and Eloquence, or The Arte of Wooing and Complimenting*, when he makes the dancing master say, " Ladies, will you be pleased to dance a country dance or two, for 'tis that which makes you truly sociable, and us truly happy ; being like the chorus of a song where all the parts sing together."

It is a moot point whether or not the Morris owes anything to Moorish or other foreign influences. No such question, however, arises with the Country Dance, which is wholly and demonstrably English. This, it is true, has been disputed even by English writers, who, deceived by a false etymology, have sometimes derived it from the French *contredanse*. This "brilliant anachronism" has been effectually refuted by Chappell and others, by a reference to dates. They have shown that the *contredanse* cannot be traced back further than the seventeenth or early eighteenth centuries; and that it is not even mentioned by Thoinot Arbeau (1589), or by any of the early French writers on dancing. On the other hand Weaver, in *An Essay towards an History of Dancing* (1712), p. 170, says, "Country dances . . . . . . is a dancing the peculiar growth of this nation, tho' now transplanted into almost all the Courts of Europe ; and is become in the most august assemblies the favourite diversion. This dancing is a moderate and healthful exercise, a pleasant and innocent diversion, if modestly used and performed at convenient times, and by suitable company." Essex, too, in his *Treatise on Chorography, or the art of dancing Country Dances* (1710), writes, "This which we call Country Dancing is originally the product of this nation."

The evidence is quite conclusive. So far from deriving our Country Dances from France, it was the French who adapted one particular form of the English dance, known as "A square dance for eight," developed it, called it *contredanse*, and sent it back to England, where in the Quadrille, one of its numerous varieties, it still survives.*

* Later on, apparently, the English Quadrille came into competition with the *contredanse* in France, for "The Times" of Jan. 12, 1820, contains the following paragraph :—"It would appear that *Contredanses* are revived in Paris, to the discountenance of Quadrilles. A collection of 500 *Contredanses* are about to be published, says the ' Journal des Modes.' "

Although the Country Dance originated with the unlettered classes it has not always been their exclusive possession. Just as the folk-songs were at one time freely sung by all classes of the community, so the Country Dances were once performed at Court and in fashionable ball-rooms, as well as on the village green. In the reign of James I. it was said that it was easier to put on fine clothes than to learn the French dances, and that therefore "none but Country Dances" must be used at Court. This, however, never became the invariable practice. The custom seems to have been to begin the ball with the more formal and, for the most part, foreign dances, e.g., the Courante, Pavane, Gavotte, and so forth, and afterwards to indulge in the merrier and less restrained Country Dance; just as, up to a few years ago, it was customary to finish the evening with the popular " Sir Roger." Dancers of the present day might do worse than revert to this old habit and substitute for the Quadrille and Lancers one or more examples of the more ancient and far more sociable Country Dance.

The dances and tunes in this book have been collected in Warwickshire, Derbyshire, Devonshire, Somerset and Surrey. It will be noticed that, like " Sir Roger," they are all danced in the familiar formation of two parallel straight lines, men on one side, women on the other. This is what was called in the old dancing books "Longways for as many as will," and it is the only formation in which, apparently, the Country Dance is performed by the country folk of the present day. But this was not always so. Playford's *English Dancing Master* (1658—1725) and other similar publications contain many dances directed to be performed in other ways. There are the Rounds for "four or eight dancers " or " for as many as will "; the " square dance for eight," already mentioned as the prototype of the Quadrille; while in the once popular "Dargason" the performers started in a single straight line, the men and women in different groups. Many of these older dances are extremely interesting, and some of them, deciphered from the old dancing books, will be described in the second part of this work.

It is impossible to close this chapter without reference to the revival of folk-dancing in England, which has lately attracted some attention.

The revival, it should be pointed out, is not peculiar to this country. A similar movement is being prosecuted with a like enthusiasm in the United States of America, as well as in certain European countries. The movement has, no doubt, for its chief objective the quickening of the national spirit, and this will most certainly be one of its immediate and most beneficent effects. But there are other motives as well. Educationists, for instance, advocate folk-dancing in schools for the sake of the physical exercise that it promotes under the guise of recreation, seeing in it a corrective to the "hockey walk," the "rowing slouch" and the wooden stiffness of bearing induced by military drill.

The movement in England has of course its critics. There are those, for instance, who point out that the primitive race which evolved the folk-dance is now in a state of decadence. Starting from this premiss, which is quite unassailable, they then proceed to argue, very illogically, that for this reason the dances themselves are decadent; that they are out of tune with the spirit of the present day and deserve nothing better than to be relegated to the lumber room together with other old and useless products of a past age.

Others, however, attracted by the simple, rhythmic beauty of their movements, and of the tunes to which they are allied, think that these ancient national dances are on their own merits far too good to be lost, and advocate wholeheartedly their revival and practice, particularly in the schools and by young people.

Among those who take this latter view must now be reckoned the Educational Authorities, who, in their new *Syllabus of Physical Exercises*, propose that the Morris and Country Dances shall forthwith be placed in the curriculum of the elementary school.

The official recognition thus accorded to the educational value of our two national dances marks a new and almost revolutionary departure, and discloses a vista full of interesting possibilities. If, however, the scheme is to yield the best and the fullest of results, it must be administered with caution and wisdom. It is, for instance, of paramount importance that the dances should be translated into the schools as accurately as possible in their native and traditional forms ; otherwise, their educational as well as their artistic value will be seriously discounted. To do this effectively will need an adequate supply of trained teachers and a staff of qualified inspectors.

Teachers, too, must realise the very different qualities which characterize, respectively, the Morris and the Country Dance, if they are to assign to each its own proper place in the educational scheme.

The Morris is the more difficult dance of the two. Its especial purpose in education is the development of physical qualities. Its movements are strong, vigorous, at times almost violent, and demand great agility and flexibility of limb. Nevertheless, they must be executed easily and gracefully and without apparent effort or physical distress ; and the ability to do this can only be acquired by constant and assiduous practice under expert supervision. Vigour under complete control is the dominant note of the Morris Dance, as it is also its chief claim to educational recognition. The greatest care must be exercised lest, on the one hand, the dance degenerate into a disorderly romp, or, on the other hand, curbed by too rigid a restraint, it become tame and lifeless. Much drill and discipline, too, will be needed if the performers are to keep their lines straight and even, and to maintain the prescribed distances from each other. Finally, it must be borne in mind that the Morris is not so much a social, recreative dance as a physical exercise, and a very strenuous one.

The Country Dance is a quieter, more reposeful dance. It is more easily learned, and is physically far less exacting than the Morris. It is, primarily, a social recreative diversion, in which both sexes take part; a homely, intimate, and above all a mannered dance. By its means many valuable lessons may be inculcated—in grace of manner and dignified behaviour, especially between the sexes; in the art of moving easily and naturally, and maintaining a fair presence and courtly bearing. In the words already quoted, the Country Dance is " a moderate and healthful exercise, a pleasant and innocent diversion, if modestly used and performed at convenient times and by suitable company."

So far, we have considered the educational worth of the folk-dance as a physical exercise only. But it is something more than this. It is an art, and a highly expressive one; an art, too, like music, to which children are peculiarly responsive. On this ground alone its introduction into the schools may be justified : for, educationally speaking, the quickening of the artistic sense is at least as important as the developing of muscles. Consequently, in placing folk-dances in the schools we are, or should be, introducing not merely a pleasurable form of physical exercise. but an art, something that is at once healthful, beautiful, and expressive. No one who has closely studied the best folk-dancing in England would hesitate for one moment to dignify it by the name of an art, nor deny that it seems to give to those who practise it an ease of manner and an air of refinement which are very attractive. It is something more than mere senti- mentality that would connect the upright bearing of the Morris dancer with the uprightness of his character. To those whose experience is limited to the cake-walks and skirt-dances of the music-hall, or to the monotonous circlings and " kitchen " lancers of the drawing-room, this view may seem fantastic. But this is only because dancing has in our time become so debased that most of us have forgotten that it is one of the most elemental and universal of the fine arts.

Ease of manner, grace and dignity of carriage, upright bearing, and so forth, can scarcely be said to distinguish the age we live in. And yet it is not so very long ago since "the dancing English" were renowned for "carrying a fair presence." Is it too much to hope that, with the revival of folk-dancing in the schools, these very desirable qualities may in the next generation once again be characteristic of the English nation?

THE DANCE.

The Country Dance is performed by any equal numbers of men and women, not fewer than six in all. The performers take partners and stand in two parallel lines, the men on one side facing the women on the other, each dancer standing opposite his or her partner. This formation is called the *General Set* and is depicted in the following diagram (□ = woman; ○ = man) :—

GENERAL SET.

WOMEN'S SIDE.

TOP.

□   □   □   □ ·· □

BOTTOM.

○   ○   ○   ○ ·· ○

MEN'S SIDE.

The distance between the lines should be approximately five feet, and between the couples about two and a half feet. The top of the General Set is that end which is nearest the music, and, if there be one, the audience; it is on the right of the women, and on the left of the men.

A Country Dance consists of an indefinite number of repetitions of a series of figures, which vary both in number and character in different dances. This series of figures is called the *complete figure*: while the subsidiary movements of which it is compounded are called *ordinary figures* or *figures*. Each performance of the complete figure is called a *round*.

Country Dance figures are very numerous. They vary in length, character, and the number of dancers that take part in their performance. Every complete figure, however, must contain, *inter alia*, what is called a *progressive figure*, the effect of which is to change the order and position of some or all of the couples. Consequently, as the dance proceeds, the couples are continually changing places, in an ordered way, some moving up and others down the General Set.

This progressive movement is the essential and distinctive, as it is the invariable, feature of the Country Dance. As an artistic device, its function is to link together and so give continuity to what would otherwise be a series of disconnected and monotonous repetitions.

There are two ways in which the progressive movement is effected, giving rise to two different types of dance. These we will call, respectively, the *whole-set* and the *minor-set* dance. The whole-set dance, as the simpler of the two, will first engage our attention.

THE WHOLE-SET DANCE.

In dances of this species the progressive movement is effected by the transference of the first couple from the top to the bottom of the General Set. With every round, therefore, each couple (with the exception of the one at the top) moves up one place, and continues this movement, step by step, until it reaches the top of the General Set, when, after the next round, it is transferred to the bottom, to resume once again its upward progress. "Sir Roger de Coverley" is a good example of this type of dance.

This is a very simple movement, as the following diagram will show.

PROGRESSIVE MOVEMENT IN A WHOLE-SET COUNTRY DANCE.

A, B, C, D, &c., are the couples. The top of the General Set is on the left hand. The numbers in the column on the left record the successive rounds or performances of the complete figure.

1.	A	B	C	D	E	F	G	H
2.	B	C	D	E	F	G	H	A
3.	C	D	E	F	G	H	A	B
4.	D	E	F	G	H	A	B	C
5.	E	F	G	H	A	B	C	D
6.	F	G	H	A	B	C	D	E
7.	G	H	A	B	C	D	E	F
8.	H	A	B	C	D	E	F	G
9.	A	B	C	D	E	F	G	H

A, which is called the *leading couple*, is now in the position it was in when the dance began. This usually brings the dance to a conclusion.

THE MINOR-SET DANCE.

In a minor-set dance the figures are performed simultaneously by subsidiary sets or groups of two, or sometimes three, adjacent couples. There are, therefore, no figures in a minor-set dance which cannot be danced by two or, at the most, three couples. The progressive figure is invariably performed by the first and second of these couples, and results in the transposition of their respective positions.

These subsidiary groups of dancers are called *minor-sets—duple* or *triple* according to the number of couples they contain. The several couples of a minor-set are called, counting from the top, *first, second* and *third* respectively.

Of these, the first couple is the chief one. It moves one step down the General Set every round, and becomes the first couple of a new minor-set in the following round. The function of the second and third couples is to aid the first one in the performance of the several figures. This they may do by remaining stationary, in which case they are called *passive*; or by actively co-operating in the performance of one or more of the figures, when they are said to be *active*. The third couple is always passive in the progressive figure.

A couple that is superfluous, that is one that is not attached to any minor-set throughout a complete round, is called a *neutral* couple. Every couple on reaching the top or the bottom of the General Set remains neutral during the next round, and sometimes the following one as well.

We are now in a position to describe the progressive movement of a dance of this description. We will begin with one divided into duple minor-sets.

Progressive Movement in a Country Dance divided into Duple Minor-Sets.

The top minor-set, headed by the leading couple, opens the dance by performing the complete figure, the rest of the couples being neutral. This results in an exchange of positions between the leading and the second couple.

The second round is now danced by the minor-set composed of the second and third couples, of which the second one is the leading couple. The rest of the dancers, including the top couple, remain neutral. This brings the leading couple down to the third place from the top of the General Set.

In the third round two minor-sets will now participate, namely, those consisting, respectively, of the two couples at the top (the second and third of the original set), and of the third and fourth couples (originally the first and fourth).

The dance proceeds in this way, the leading couple gradually moving down the General Set and bringing into action after each round one new couple, and after every second round a fresh minor-set. When, therefore, the leading couple has reached the second place from the bottom of the General Set, all the couples (with the possible exception of the top one) will be actively engaged, and will continue to be so until the dance is concluded.

The progressive movement above described is shown in the following diagram.

Neutral couples are placed between parentheses, and minor-sets within square brackets.

1.	[A B]	(C)	(D)	(E)	(F)	(G)
2.	(B)	[A C]	(D)	(E)	(F)	(G)
3.	[B C]	[A D]	(E)	(F)	(G)	
4.	(C)	[B D]	[A E]	(F)	(G)	
5.	[C D]	[B E]	[A F]	(G)		
6.	(D)	[C E]	[B F]	[A G]		
7.	[D E]	[C F]	[B G]	(A)		
8.	(E)	[D F]	[C G]	[B A]		
9.	[E F]	[D G]	[C A]	(B)		

From the above diagram it will be seen that each couple, on arriving at either end of the General Set, remains neutral during the following round. When, therefore, as in the above example, the number of couples is uneven, there will always be one neutral couple in every round, alternately at the top and bottom of the General Set.

If, however, the number of couples be even, there will be alternately (1) *no* neutral couple, and (2) *two* neutral couples (one at each end). This is shown in the following diagram :—

7.	[D E]	[C F]	[B G]	[A H]
8.	(E)	[D F]	[C G]	[B H] (A)
9.	[E F]	[D G]	[C H]	[B A]
10.	(F)	[E G]	[D H]	[C A] (B)

Progressive Movement in a Country Dance divided into Triple Minor-Sets.

The progression of the couples in a triple minor-set dance, although governed by the same principle, is both in theory and practice rather more complicated. The movement is shown in the following diagram :—

1.	[A	B	C]	(D)	(E)	(F)	(G)	(H)
2.	(B)	[A	C	D]	(E)	(F)	(G)	(H)
3.	(B)	(C)	[A	D	E]	(F)	(G)	(H)
4.	[B	C	D]	[A	E	F]	(G)	(H)
5.	(C)	[B	D	E]	[A	F	G]	(H)
6.	(C)	(D)	[B	E	F]	[A	G	H]
7.	[C	D	E]	[B	F	G]	[A	H]
8.	(D)	[C	E	F]	[B	G	H]	(A)
9.	(D)	(E)	[C	F	G]	[B	H	A]
10.	[D	E	F]	[C	G	H]	[B	A]
11.	(E)	[D	F	G]	[C	H	A]	(B)
12.	(E)	(F)	[D	G	H]	[C	A	B]
13.	[E	F	G]	[D	H	A]	[C	B]
14.	(F)	[E	G	H]	[D	A	B]	(C)

Attention is directed to the following points :—

1. A couple going down the dance moves a step each round.
2. A couple going up moves a step in every alternate round only. It therefore takes twice as long to go up as to go down the General Set.
3. Each couple takes the last step to the bottom as the first couple of a duple instead of a triple minor-set (see rounds 7, 10, 13). The two couples of this incomplete minor-set will, of course, be unable to

perform, without modification, those figures which require the co-operation of three couples ; but they will always be able to execute the progressive figure, which is the essential one.

4. Each couple upon reaching the top of the General Set remains there as a neutral couple for the two following rounds.

5. Each couple upon reaching the bottom of the General Set remains neutral for the next round only.

The number of neutral couples, and their disposition in the successive rounds, depend upon the total number of couples engaged in the dance. If, as in the above example, this number when divided by three leaves a remainder of two couples, then, as we have seen, the neutral couples will be successively **(1)** *none*, **(2)** *two* (one at each end), and **(3)** *two* (both at the top).

On the other hand, if the total number of couples is exactly divisible by three, the numbers of neutral couples will be **(1)** *none*, **(2)** *one* (at the top), and **(3)** *three* (one at the lower end and two at the upper), as shown in the following diagram :—

7.	[C	D	E]	[B	F	G]	[A	H	L]
8.	(D)	[C	E	F]	[B	G	H]	[A	L]
9.	(D)	(E)	[C	F	G]	[B	H	L]	(A)
10.	[D	E	F]	[C	G	H]	[B	L	A]

And lastly, when there is only one odd couple, the neutral couples work out as follows :—**(1)** *one* (at the top), **(2)** *two* (both at the top), and **(3)** *one* (at the bottom). This is shown in the following diagram :—

5.	(C)	[B	D	E]	[A	F	G]
6.	(C)	(D)	[B	E	F]	[A	G]
7.	[C	D	E]	[B	F	G]	(A)
8.	(D)	[C	E	F]	[B	G	A]

A minor-set dance is, of course, much more difficult to perform neatly than a whole-set dance. To avoid confusion each couple must, at the beginning of every round, be quite clear to which minor-set it belongs, and its position in that set. Active couples, moreover, should be very careful to confine their movements within the limits of their own minor-set, and thus avoid encroaching upon the space occupied by the minor-sets on either side. If these two recommendations are scrupulously observed, a smooth and orderly performance will be ensured.

Expert dancers will sometimes constitute themselves into minor-sets for the performance of the first round, and thus avoid the gradual and somewhat tedious opening as above described; that is to say, they will omit the first six rounds in our first illustration and begin with the seventh round.

STEPS AND FIGURES.

THE STEPS.

The steps used in the traditional Country Dance are few in number and simple in execution. When, in its later developments, the dance became popular in polite society, the usual steps, *e.g.*, the chassé, assemblé, jetté, etc., were used and taught by the fashionable dancing masters. But these steps do not properly belong to the traditional dance, though possibly they may originally have been derived therefrom. Country folk never point the toe, arch the leg, attitudinize, or affect a swaying or mincing gait. Movements of this kind are quite alien to the spirit of the Country Dance, which is one of rustic jollity and simple good humour rather than of conventional elegance.

It may indeed be questioned whether the country dancer ever concerns himself, consciously at any rate, with the steps he is dancing. His interest and attention are absorbed in the figures, and in the execution of the progressive movement. This he shows in the extraordinary care he will take to keep his right position, to move in time with the music, and to begin and end each figure precisely with the opening and closing bars of the strain of the music to which it belongs.

The normal Country Dance step is a springy walking step, two to each bar—executed by the women with a natural, unaffected grace, and on the part of men with a complacent bearing and a certain jauntiness of manner which is very difficult to describe, and which must, perhaps, be seen to be appreciated.

The galop, waltz and polka steps are occasionally used, and there are, in addition, certain steps which are prescriptive in particular figures. These will be indicated and, where necessary, described in the notation of the dances. It must be understood, however, that when no step is specifically mentioned the normal walking step is to be used.

Some of the steps given in the music diagrams in the notation may, at first sight, look very similar to certain steps used in the Morris Dance. The likeness, however, is only superficial. The steps in the Country Dance are performed very smoothly and quietly; the feet should slide where possible, and, if raised, should not be lifted more than two or three inches from the ground; while the raised leg must never be thrust forward as in the typical Morris step.

THE FIGURES.

The number of figures that are known to have been used at one time or another in the history of the Country Dance is very large; and this means that the number of possible varieties of the Country Dance is practically infinite. For any series of figures, combined in accordance with the theory of the dance and in conformity with the structure of the tune, will constitute a complete figure. With two exceptions, "The Triumph" and "Sir Roger de Coverley," each of which is invariably danced in its own way and to its own tune, not a single one of the innumerable varieties of the Country Dance has ever been recognised, except perhaps locally, as a fixed and distinct dance.

It should be mentioned that when the Country Dance was performed in the ball-room it was the custom for the leading couple to have the "call," that is, the privilege of naming the tune and prescribing the figures. It was necessary, therefore, for expert dancers of those days to be proficient not only in the performance of the dance but in the theory as well. For the benefit of those who were unable to make the "call" numerous publications were issued from the 17th century onwards, containing Country Dance airs, together with the descriptions of the figures, though not of the steps, that were to be danced to them. Similar descriptions, but with the names only of the tunes to which they were to be performed, were also often printed on the fly-leaves of pocket-books and diaries of the 18th and early 19th centuries. Usually, though not invariably, the name of the dance was derived from that of the tune.

The figures which are now to be explained represent a few only of those that are still in use in the country districts. They include, however, all of those which occur in one or other of the dances presently to be described. First, however, it will be necessary to explain the meaning of certain technical terms, symbols, expressions, &c., that will be used in the notation :—

1. The term " lead " is used when partners move up or down the dance *with joined hands*.

2. To " move " is an expression which is applied to individual dancers, or to partners with unlinked hands, when the movement takes place *between the lines of the General Set*.

3. To " cast off " is to turn outwards and proceed without one or other of the lines of the dancers ; to " cast up " or " cast down " is to dance up or down outside the General Set.

4. Two adjacent couples are said to " cast one " when, at the end of a movement, they exchange positions.

5. To " cross hands " the man takes the right and left hands of his partner with his right and left hands respectively, the right hands being uppermost. The hands are sometimes though rarely, crossed behind the backs of the dancers.

In the diagrams the positions of the women are shown, as hitherto, by squares, and those of the men by circles ; while the paths of the women are indicated by dotted lines, and those of the men by ordinary lines.

When music diagrams are used to explain the steps, R stands for *right foot*, L for *left foot*, and H for *hop*.

FIGURE 1.

Swing or Set.

(Eight bars.)

Partners meet, engage in waltz fashion, and dance round in a small circle between the lines of the General Set. At the beginning of the last bar they disengage, return to places, and bow to each other.

The step varies with the rhythm of the music, and may take any one of the three following forms: (1) The waltz step; (2) the polka step or a modification of it; (3) step and hop on alternate feet.

Country dancers sometimes, though very rarely, substitute for the Swing the more conventional *Set* or *Set-to-partners*, a figure which is familiar to all quadrille dancers. This was the invariable custom in the ball-room where the Swing, as above described, was quite unknown.

There was, however, a figure known to fashionable dancers as the Swing, but this was performed in quite another manner: Partners met, joined right hands, turned slowly round from right to left and returned to places.

In the notation the term Swing may be interpreted in any one of these three ways. The first method, which is also the traditional one, will probably be found the most suitable.

FIGURE 2.

First couple swings down the middle and takes up position below the last couple.

(Eight bars.)

The first couple swings slowly down the middle, while each of the other couples moves up one place. The first couple, on reaching the bottom of the General Set, takes the position just vacated by the last couple (eight bars). This is a progressive figure, and is performed in whole-set dances only.

FIGURE 3.

FIRST AND SECOND COUPLES SWING AND CAST ONE.

(Eight bars.)

First and second couples swing at the same time, taking care not to obstruct each other. At the end of the figure they exchange positions, the top couple moving down one place, and the second couple moving up one place.

This is a progressive figure.

FIGURE 4.

FIRST COUPLE LEADS DOWN THE MIDDLE AND BACK AGAIN.

(Eight bars.)

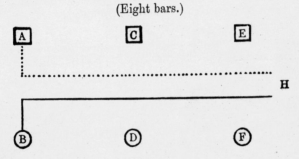

The first woman and the first man, A and B, join and raise left hands and lead down the middle to H (four bars). They then release hands, turn round and, right hand in right hand, lead up to the top. Here they separate, return to places, and bow to each other (four bars).

The turn at H is sometimes performed in the following way:—B, with his left hand, raises his partner's left hand above her head, turns her round under it, and then leads her up to the top with crossed hands.

The traditional walking step is generally used in leading down, but in leading up a more lively step is customary.

In a whole-set dance A and B will lead down to the bottom of the General Set, or as far as time will allow; but in a minor-set dance they must be careful not to cause confusion by going more than a few steps at the most beyond the limits of their own minor set.

FIGURE 5.

THE FIRST COUPLE LEADS DOWN THE MIDDLE AND BACK AGAIN
AND CASTS ONE.

(Eight bars.)

The first couple leads down the middle in the way described in the last figure (four bars). While this movement is in progress the second couple moves up one place. The first couple on reaching the top of the General Set takes the position previously held by the second couple (four bars).

This is a progressive figure.

FIGURE 6.

FIRST MAN AND FIRST WOMAN LEAD DOWN THE MIDDLE AND
BACK AGAIN AND THROUGH THE TOP COUPLE.

(Eight bars.)

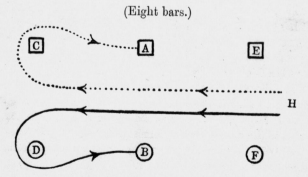

This is a variant of the preceding figure. A and B, on returning up the middle, instead of proceeding at once to the places just vacated by the second couple, lead up to the top, release hands, cast off, pass round and outside C and D respectively, and proceed to their new positions as in the last figure (eight bars).

This is a progressive figure.

FIGURE 7.

"STEP AND FETCH HER," WITH FIRST COUPLE AND SECOND MAN.

(Eight bars.)

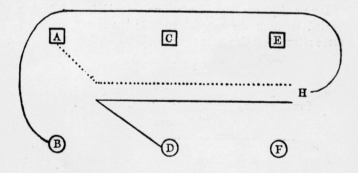

D and A meet and lead down the middle to H. At the same time B crosses over and casts round A, C, and E. All three meet at H (four bars).

B now displaces D, crosses hands with A, and leads her up the middle, D, with hang-dog expression, following disconsolately. All three return to their original places (four bars).

FIGURE 8.

"STEP AND FETCH HER," WITH SECOND COUPLE AND
FIRST MAN.

(Eight bars.)

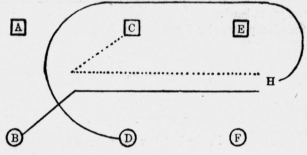

B and C meet and lead down the middle to H, while D
crosses over and casts round C and E.   All three meet at H
(four bars).

D now displaces B and leads C up the middle, B following
behind them in the way described in the last figure.   All
three return to their places (four bars).

FIGURE 9.

"THE TRIUMPH," WITH FIRST COUPLE AND SECOND MAN.

(Eight bars.)

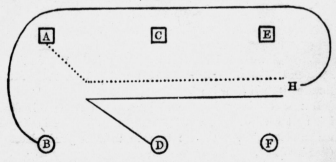

D meets A and leads her down the middle to H. During this movement B crosses over and casts round A, C, and E. All three meet at H (four bars).

D and B stand on the left and right of A respectively.

D and A join left hands, while B and A join right hands. D with his right hand takes the left hand of B.

The two men, B and D, raise their joined hands above A's head and lead her "in triumph" up the middle to the top, where all three separate and return to their proper places (four bars).

FIGURE 10.

"THE TRIUMPH," WITH SECOND COUPLE AND FIRST MAN.

(Eight bars.)

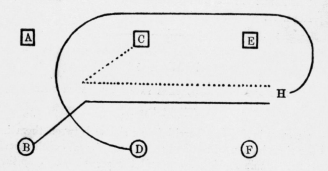

B and C meet and lead down the middle to H. Simultaneously D crosses over and casts round C and E. All three meet at H (four bars).

The two men, B and D, now lead C "in triumph" up the middle as in the last figure (four bars).

FIGURE 11.

Hands across with first and second couples.

(Eight bars.)

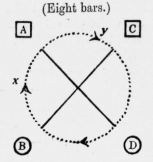

B and C join right hands. D and A do the same. All four dance round in the direction *x y* (four bars).

They then release and change hands, dance round in the reverse direction and return to places (four bars).

A and D have their hands uppermost.

The hands should be held up as high as the faces of the performers.

FIGURE 12.

First and second couples pass under four times.

(Eight bars.)

Partners hold a handkerchief or a ribbon between them in their right hands. First and second couples face each other, the first couple looking down and the second couple up the General Set.

The first couple then moves down three short steps, raising right arms and making an arch with the handkerchief. At the same time, the second couple moves up three steps, passing under the arch made by the first couple (two bars).

The second couple now moves down three steps, making an arch, under which the first couple passes up, taking three steps as before (two bars).

This double movement is then repeated, after which the dancers separate and return to places (four bars).

FIGURE 13.

First woman and second man advance, bow, turn round, and swing.

(Eight bars.)

The first woman and the second man advance a step or two towards each other. The woman curtseys and the man bows, after which they both turn round slowly without moving from their respective positions (four bars).

They advance, meet, swing and return to places (four bars).

The first half of this movement must be performed with great deliberation.

FIGURE 14.

First man and second woman advance, bow, turn round, and swing.

(Eight bars.)

The first man and the second woman advance. The man bows, the woman curtseys, and then each turns slowly round without moving from position (four bars).

They meet, swing, and return to places (four bars).

FIGURE 15.

FIGURE EIGHT BY FIRST MAN.
(Eight bars.)

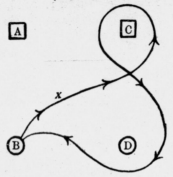

B advances along line **x**, passes round the right of C, then round the left of D and back to position (eight bars).

FIGURE 16.

FIGURE EIGHT BY FIRST WOMAN.
(Eight bars.)

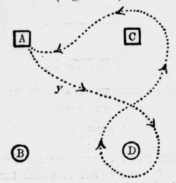

A advances along line **y**, passes round the left of D, then round the right of C and back to position (eight bars).

FIGURE 17.

FIGURE EIGHT BY FIRST MAN AND FIRST WOMAN.

(Eight bars.)

The two preceding figures are performed simultaneously by first man and first woman. The man must be careful to allow the woman to pass in front of him.

FIGURE 18.

FIRST COUPLE SEPARATES AND CASTS OFF, FOLLOWED BY ALL THE COUPLES EXCEPT THE LAST ONE. PARTNERS MEET BELOW THE LAST COUPLE, PASS SUCCESSIVELY UNDER AN ARCH MADE BY LAST COUPLE, LEAD UP AND RETURN TO THEIR RESPECTIVE PLACES.

(Eight bars.)

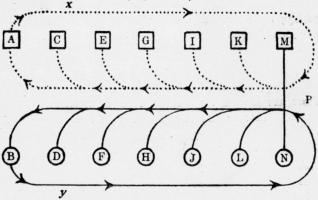

A casts off along dotted line *x*, followed by C, E, G, &c.

B casts off along line *y*, followed by D, F, H, &c.

A and B meet at P, join right hands, pass under an arch made by M and N, and lead up the middle to their proper places, followed by all the other couples.

C, E, G, &c., and D, F, H, &c., before casting off, proceed, not necessarily to the top of the General Set, but as far as the time of the music will allow.

FIGURE 19.

Fɪʀsᴛ ᴄᴏᴜᴘʟᴇ ᴠɪsɪᴛs sᴇᴄᴏɴᴅ ᴡᴏᴍᴀɴ ᴀɴᴅ sᴇᴄᴏɴᴅ ᴍᴀɴ.

(Eight bars.)

First couple, with joined hands, moves down and faces second woman. The two women curtsey while the man bows (four bars).

The first couple turns and faces second man, with whom similar courtesies are exchanged. They then separate and return to places (four bars).

FIGURE 20.

Fɪʀsᴛ ᴄᴏᴜᴘʟᴇ ʟɪɴᴋs ᴀʀᴍs ᴀɴᴅ sᴡɪɴɢs ʀᴏᴜɴᴅ.

(Four bars.)

Partners advance and meet. They link right or left arms, according to instructions, and facing in opposite directions, swing round, separate and return to places (four bars).

FIGURE 21.

Fɪʀsᴛ ᴍᴀɴ ᴀɴᴅ ғɪʀsᴛ ᴡᴏᴍᴀɴ ᴍᴏᴠᴇ ᴅᴏᴡɴ ᴛʜᴇ ᴍɪᴅᴅʟᴇ ᴀɴᴅ ᴄᴀsᴛ ᴜᴘ ᴛʜʀᴏᴜɢʜ ᴛʜᴇ ᴛʜɪʀᴅ ᴄᴏᴜᴘʟᴇ.

(Eight bars.)

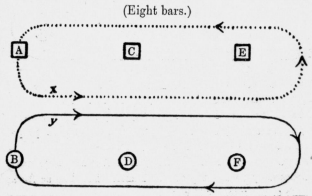

A moves down the middle along the dotted line *x* (four bars), casts off round the third woman E and returns to position (four bars).

Simultaneously, B moves down the middle along the line *y* (four bars), casts off round the third man F and returns to position as shown in diagram (four bars).

FIGURE 22.

FIRST AND SECOND COUPLES CROSS OVER, TURN ROUND AND CROSS BACK AGAIN.

(Eight bars.)

First and second couples cross over, each man passing on the left of his partner (two bars).

All four dancers turn round and face each other (two bars).

The movement is then repeated in reverse, the men passing on the right of their partners (four bars). This brings all four dancers back to places.

FIGURE 23.

MEN AND WOMEN ADVANCE, RETIRE, AND CROSS OVER; AND THEN REPEAT MOVEMENT IN REVERSE.

(Sixteen bars.)

Men and women advance, meet and bow (two bars). They then retire to places (two bars).

Men cross over to women's side, and women cross over to men's side, each man passing on the left of his partner (two bars).

All turn round and face partners (two bars).

These movements are then repeated in reverse, the men passing on the right of their partners. This brings all the dancers back to places (eight bars).

Sometimes the men link arms and the women join hands in advancing and retiring.

FIGURE 24.

FIRST COUPLE, WITH CROSSED HANDS, CASTS OFF AND LEADS
UP THE MIDDLE TO POSITION, FOLLOWED BY ALL THE
OTHER COUPLES.

(Eight bars.)

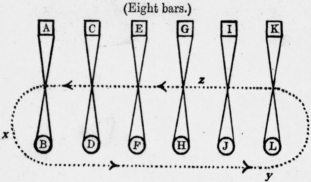

All partners cross hands and follow A and B, who cast off
in the line **x y**, lead up the middle along the line **z**, and
return to position (eight bars).

FIGURE 25.

FIRST MAN AND FIRST WOMAN CAST OFF, PASS THROUGH THE
THIRD COUPLE, LEAD UP THE MIDDLE AND FACE THE
SECOND COUPLE.

(Eight bars.)

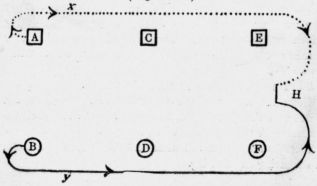

A casts off in line *x* and B casts off in line *y*. They meet at H (four bars). During this movement, C and D move up into the places just vacated by A and B.

A and B now lead up the middle (four bars), C and D with joined hands meeting and facing them at the top, thus :—

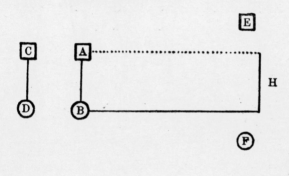

FIGURE 26.

SECOND AND FIRST COUPLES, FACE TO FACE, MOVE DOWN THE MIDDLE AND UP AGAIN ; THE FIRST COUPLE PASSES UNDER.

(Eight bars.)

C and D face A and B, as shown in the last diagram of the preceding figure. All four move down the middle to H, C and D forwards, A and B backwards (four bars).

The two couples then return up the middle, A and B forwards, C and D backwards. When they have nearly reached the top, C and D raise their joined hands, under which A and B pass. All four return to their original places (four bars).

Partners join right hands throughout this figure.

FIGURE 27.

HANDS THREE ON THE WOMEN'S SIDE : FIRST WOMAN
PASSES UNDER.

(Eight bars.)

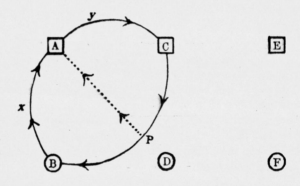

A, B and C join hands and dance once round in a ring in
the direction **x y** (four bars).

They continue dancing in the same direction for another
half circle, when A will be at P (two bars).

B and C then raise their joined hands, under which A
passes to her place (two bars).

It is important that the passing under the arch should
occur exactly on the first beat of the seventh bar of the
music.

FIGURE 28.

HANDS THREE ON THE MEN'S SIDE : SECOND MAN PASSES UNDER

(Eight bars.)

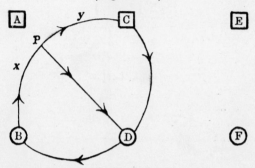

B, C and D join hands and dance once round in a ring in the direction **x y** (four bars).

They continue dancing round in the same direction for another half circle, when D will be at P (two bars). B and C then raise their joined hands under which D passes to his place (two bars).

This figure follows the preceding one without pause.

FIGURE 29.

FIRST COUPLE TURNS ; SECOND WOMAN PASSES UNDER TO FIRST PLACE.

(Eight bars.)

First man and first woman join and raise their right hands and dance round in a small circle between the lines of the General Set. On the first note of the seventh bar of the music they must be exactly opposite the second woman. The latter quickly passes under the arch to the place just vacated by the first woman (eight bars).

This is a progressive figure.

FIGURE 30.

FIRST COUPLE TURNS; SECOND MAN PASSES UNDER
TO FIRST PLACE.

(Eight bars.)

First man and first woman continue to dance round in the
way described in the last figure. On the first note of the
seventh bar the second man passes quickly under the arch
and takes the place previously occupied by the first man.

First man and first woman return to places just vacated by
second man and second woman (eight bars).

This figure, which is a progressive one, follows upon the
preceding one without pause.

FIGURE 31.

THE FIRST WOMAN MOVES DOWN AND BACK, AND CASTS DOWN
AND BACK; WHILE THE FIRST MAN CASTS DOWN AND
BACK, AND MOVES DOWN AND BACK.

(Sixteen bars.)

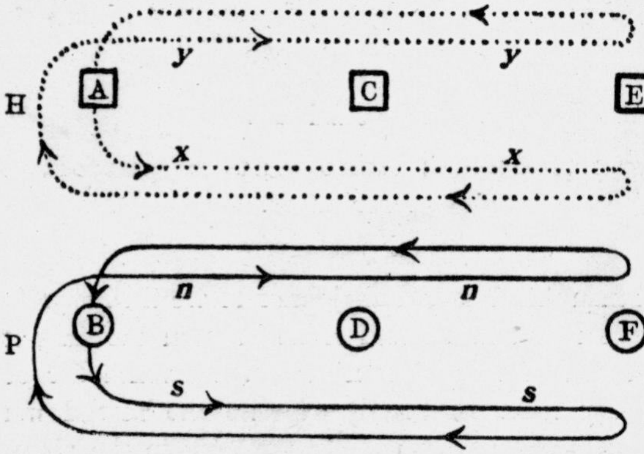

The first woman A moves down the line *x* as far as the
third woman E (four bars) and then moves *backwards* to the

top (four bars). At H she raises both arms above her head, turns completely round from left to right, casts down in line *y* as far as E (four bars), and then moves backwards to her place (four bars).

Simultaneously, the first man B casts down in the line *s* as far as the third man F (four bars), and then moves backwards to the top (four bars). At P he raises both arms above his head, turns completely round from left to right, moves down the middle along the line *n* as far as F (four bars), and then returns backwards to position (four bars).

FIGURE 32.

HANDS FOUR WITH FIRST AND SECOND COUPLES.

(Eight bars.)

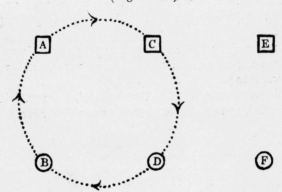

A, B, C, and D join hands and dance round in a ring from left to right (four bars). *clockwise*

They then repeat the movement in the reverse direction, separate, and return to places (four bars).

FIGURE 33.

THREE MEET.

(Eight bars.)

First, second and third men link arms. First, second and third women do the same.

The men and women, taking two short steps to each bar, advance towards each other till they meet (two bars).

They then move backwards and return to places (two bars). This double movement is then repeated (four bars).

FIGURE 34.

DOUBLE CHANGE SIDES WITH FIRST AND SECOND COUPLES.

(Eight bars.)

First and second women join right hands, cross over to men's side (two bars) and retire backwards to places (two bars).

Simultaneously, first and second men cross over to women's side, passing on either side of the two women, and retire backwards to places (four bars).

This double movement is then repeated, the men joining right hands and passing between the women (four bars).

NOTATION.

BRIGHTON CAMP

Whole-Set.

MUSIC.	MOVEMENTS.
A.	First couple, with crossed hands, casts off and leads up the middle to position, followed by all the other couples. Fig. 24 (p. 40).
B1.	First couple swings down the middle and takes up position below the last couple (progressive). Fig. 2 (p. 28).
B2.	All couples swing. Fig. 1 (p. 28).

When many couples are dancing it may be necessary to repeat the music to the first figure.

All three figures are danced to the following step :—

L R L HL R L R HR

L R L HL

GALOPEDE.

WHOLE-SET.

MUSIC.	MOVEMENTS.
A1.	Men and women advance, retire and cross over. Fig. 23 (p. 39).
A2.	Movement repeated in reverse. Fig. 23 (p. 39).
B.	All couples swing. Fig. 1 (p. 28).
C.	First couple swings down the middle and takes up position below the last couple (progressive). Fig. 2 (p. 28).

In the last figure the dancers must remember to move up one place while the first couple are swinging down the middle.

The "swing" in the last two figures is danced to the following step:—

RIBBON DANCE.

Whole-Set.

MUSIC.	MOVEMENTS.
A.	First and second, third and fourth, fifth and sixth couples, &c., pass under four times. Fig. 12 (p. 34).
B1.	First couple separates and casts off, followed by all the couples except the last one. Partners meet below the last couple, pass successively under an arch made by the last couple, lead up and return to their respective places. Fig. 18 (p. 37).
B2.	First couple swings down the middle under arches made by all the other couples, and takes up position below the last couple (progressive). Fig. 2 (p. 28).

If the number of couples is uneven, the last couple will be neutral during the first figure in every round.

Partners hold a ribbon between them in their right hands. The ribbons should be three or four inches broad and may be of the same or different colours. When "casting off" in the second figure, the ribbons should be released by the women, and re-taken on meeting their partners and before passing under the arch.

The last round ends with the second figure, which is varied in the following way: The first man and the first woman, after passing under the arch, instead of proceeding to the top of the General Set, place themselves next to the last couple, and make an arch with their ribbon. The second couple then passes under the two arches, takes up a position next to the first couple, and makes an arch. The remaining couples follow suit.

When many couples are dancing it may be necessary to repeat the music to the second figure.

The " casting off " and the " swing " are danced to the following step :—

L   HL   R   HR   L   HL   R   HR   L   HL   R   HR

THE BUTTERFLY.

DUPLE MINOR-SET.

MUSIC.	MOVEMENTS.
A1.	Hands across with first and second couples. Fig. 11 (p. 34).
B.	First and second couples pass under four times. Fig. 12 (p. 34).
A2.	First and second couples swing and cast one (progressive). Fig. 3 (p. 29).

Partners hold between them, in their right hands, a handkerchief, or two handkerchiefs tied together.

The " swing " is danced to the following step :—

L   R   L   R   L   R   **L**   R   L

WE WON'T GO HOME TILL MORNING.

DUPLE MINOR-SET.

MUSIC.	MOVEMENTS.
A1.	Hands across with first and second couples. Fig. 11 (p. 34).
B1.	All the dancers stand still and clap their hands in the following rhythm ♩. ♩. | ♩. | ♩. ♩. | ♩. |, *i.e.*, on notes marked with a cross in the music.
A2.	First man and first woman lead down the middle and back again through the top couple (progressive). Fig. 6 (p. 30).
B2.	All clap as in second figure.
A3.	First and second couples swing. Fig. 1 (p. 28).

The "swing" and "leading back again" are danced to the following step :—

R HR L   HL R HR L   HL

R HR L   HL

SPEED THE PLOUGH.

Duple Minor-Set.

MUSIC.	MOVEMENTS.
A1.	First couple visits second woman and second man. Fig. 19 (p. 38).
A2.	First couple leads down the middle and back again. Fig. 4 (p. 29).
B1.	First and second couples cross over, turn round, and cross back again. Fig. 22 (p. 39).
B2.	First and second couples swing and cast one (progressive). Fig. 3 (p. 29).

In " leading back again " the galop step is used, and in the " swing " the polka step.

POP GOES THE WEASEL (First Version).

Duple Minor-Set.

MUSIC.	MOVEMENTS.
A1.	Hands three on the women's side ; first woman passes under. Fig. 27 (p. 42).
A2.	Hands three on the men's side ; second man passes under. Fig. 28 (p. 43).
B1.	First couple leads down the middle and back again. Fig. 4 (p. 29).
B2.	First and second couples swing and cast one (progressive). Fig. 3 (p. 29).

" Hands three " and " leading back again " are danced to the following step :

L   R   L   R   L   R   L   R   L   R   L   R

The " swing " is danced as follows :

L   R   L   R   L   R   L   R   L

POP GOES THE WEASEL (Second Version).

Duple Minor-Set.

MUSIC.	MOVEMENTS.
A1.	First couple turns ; second woman passes under to first place (progressive). Fig. 29 (p. 43).
A2.	First couple turns ; second man passes under to first place (progressive). Fig. 30 (p. 44).
B1.	First couple leads down the middle and back again Fig. 4 (p. 29).
B2.	First and second couples swing. Fig. 1 (p. 28).

The " swing " and " leading back again " are danced as in the first version, and the first two figures to the following step :—

L   HL   R   HR   L   HL

THE FLOWERS OF EDINBURGH.

Duple Minor-Set.

MUSIC.	MOVEMENTS.
A1.	Figure eight by first man. Fig. 15 (p. 36).
A2.	Figure eight by first woman. Fig. 16 (p. 36).
B1.	Figure eight by first man and first woman. Fig. 17 (p. 37).
B2.	First and second couples swing and cast one (progressive). Fig. 3 (p. 29).

The " swing " should be danced to the polka step.   The figure eight is danced as follows :—

The dancers take very short steps, the man stamping his feet with decision.   The woman steps more daintily, and does not stamp.

NANCY'S FANCY.

DUPLE MINOR-SET.

MUSIC.	MOVEMENTS.
A.	Double change sides with first and second couples. Fig. 34 (p. 46).
B.	First man and first woman lead down the middle and back again through the top couple (progressive). Fig. 6 (p. 30).
C.	First and second couples swing. Fig. 1 (p. 28).

The "swing" and "leading back again" are danced to the following step :—

L R L R L R L R L

BONNETS SO BLUE.

Duple Minor-Set.

MUSIC.	MOVEMENTS.
A.	Hands across with first and second couples. Fig. 11 (p. 34).
B.	First couple leads down the middle and back again and casts one (progressive). Fig. 5 (p. 30).
C.	First and second couples swing. Fig. 1 (p. 28).

"Hands across," "leading back again," and the "swing" are danced to the following step :—

L HLR HRL HLR HR L HLR HR

In "hands across" the dancers begin with the left feet and place their right feet a little in front of the left. In the second half of the figure they begin with the right feet and place the left feet in front of the right.

THE TRIUMPH.

Triple Minor-Set.

MUSIC.	MOVEMENTS.
A1.	" The Triumph " with first couple and second man. Fig. 9 (p. 32).
A2.	" The Triumph " with second couple and first man. Fig 10 (p. 33).
B.	First couple leads down the middle and back again. Fig. 4 (p. 29).
C.	First and second couples swing and cast one (progressive). Fig. 3 (p. 29).

The conventional walking step, in minim beats, is used throughout, except in the "swing" and "leading back again," which are danced to the following step :—

R HR L HL   R HR L HL   R HR L HL

STEP AND FETCH HER, OR FOLLOW YOUR LOVER.

Triple Minor-Set.

MUSIC.	MOVEMENTS.
A1.	" Step and fetch her," with first couple and second man. Fig. 7 (p. 31).
A2.	" Step and fetch her," with second couple and first man. Fig. 8 (p. 32).
B.	First couple leads down the middle and back again. Fig. 4 (p. 29).
C.	First and second couples swing and cast one (progressive). Fig. 3 (p. 29).

The " swing " and " leading back again " are danced to the following step :—

R HR   L HL   R   HR L HL   R HR   L   HL

HASTE TO THE WEDDING (First Version),

Triple Minor-Set.

MUSIC.	MOVEMENTS.
A1. and **A2.**	The first woman moves down and back, and casts down and back; while the first man casts down and back, and moves down and back. Fig. 31 (p. 44).
B1.	First couple leads down the middle and back again. Fig. 4 (p. 29).
B2.	First and second couples swing and cast one (progressive). Fig. 3 (p. 29).

" Leading back again " is danced to the galop step, and the " swing " to the following :—

L   L   R L   R   L R   L   R L

HASTE TO THE WEDDING (Second Version).

Duple Minor-Set.

MUSIC.	MOVEMENTS.
A1.	First woman and second man advance, bow, turn round and swing. Fig. 13 (p. 35).
A2.	First man and second woman advance, bow, turn round and swing. Fig. 14 (p. 35).
B1.	First couple leads down the middle and back again. Fig. 4 (p. 29).
B2.	First and second couples swing and cast one (progressive). Fig. 3 (p. 29).

The " swing " and " leading back again " are danced to the same steps as in the first version.

[handwritten: walk 8 down / 8 back — 2 under arms]

HUNT THE SQUIRREL.

[handwritten: Duple]

Triple Minor-Set.

MUSIC.	MOVEMENTS.
A1.	Hands four with first and second couples. Fig. 32 (p. 45).
B1.	First man and first woman cast off, pass through the third couple, lead up the middle and face second couple. Fig. 25 (p. 40).
A2.	Second and first couples, face to face, move down the middle and up again; the first couple passes under. Fig. 26 (p. 41).
B2.	First and second couples swing and cast one (progressive). Fig. 3 (p. 29).

[handwritten: 8 walk + 1 2 3 hop]

[handwritten: guvergh thard...]

In the third figure and in " casting off," the usual walking step is used.   " Hands four," " leading up the middle " and the " swing " are danced to the following step :—

L   HL   R   HR   L   HL   R   HR

TINK-A-TINK.

Triple Minor-Set.

MUSIC.	MOVEMENTS.
A1. Bars 1-4	First and second couples each link right arms and swing round. Fig. 20 (p. 38).
A1. Bars 5-8	First and second couples each link left arms and swing round. Fig. 20 (p. 38).
B.	First man and first woman move down the middle and cast up through the third couple. Fig. 21 (p. 38).
A2.	Hands four with first and second couples. Fig 32 (p. 45).
C.	First and second couples swing and cast one (progressive). Fig. 3 (p. 29).

The following step is used throughout the dance :—

L   HL   R   HR   L   HL   R   HR

THREE MEET, OR THE PLEASURES OF THE TOWN.

Triple Minor-Set.

MUSIC.	MOVEMENTS.
A1.	Three meet. Fig. 33 (p. 46).
A2.	First couple, with crossed hands, casts off and leads up the middle to position, followed by second and third couples. Fig. 24 (p. 40).
B1.	First man and first woman lead down the middle and back again and through the top couple (progressive). Fig. 6 (p. 30).
B2.	First and second couples swing. Fig. 1 (p. 28).

The second figure is sometimes performed by all the dancers, after the manner of a whole-set dance.

In the second figure, " leading back again " and the " swing " the following step is used :—

L   HL   R   HR   L   HL